The Goddess Frame of Mind

Eirian Naomi Omid

Published by EirianWrites Studios, 2023.

While every precaution has been taken in the preparation of this book, the publisher assumes no responsibility for errors or omissions, or for damages resulting from the use of the information contained herein.

THE GODDESS FRAME OF MIND

First edition. May 12, 2023.

Copyright © 2023 Eirian Naomi Omid.

ISBN: 979-8223384519

Written by Eirian Naomi Omid.

Dedicated to all the beautiful Goddesses out there who have forgotten their innate power. It is time to awaken that power and remember where you come from. ~ The Universe

Hello Goddess,

Welcome to the Goddess Frame of Mind.

I am EirianWrites.

I began this adventure in 2021, on a mission to spread "Goddess Mindset" to those who need it most, via a podcast called "EirianWrites and the Goddess Experience."

The podcast is still alive and well, and you can check it out by visiting the link in the back of the book.

However...

I wanted to preserve the original lessons for you, so that you can learn from my experience and grow at an accelerated rate. Hopefully managing to avoid some of my biggest pitfalls in the process.

This book was composed from the podcast manuscripts of the first episodes of *EirianWrites and the Goddess Experience*, which were written with the intent to heal trauma and help you move forward into your highest vibration of being.

This information has been shared, from me to you, for your highest and greatest good, and harming none.

In the first part of the book, you will find six chapters. Each chapter contains a useful exercise so that you may heal from your trauma and move forward in your life.

The second part of the book was specially crafted to help you unleash your divine Goddess energy through affirmations which I have created for this specific purpose.

I will also teach you how to create your own affirmations, so that you can always elevate your mindset, regardless of the cards you are handed in the moment; and teach you how to turn your affirmations into incantations to maximize their power.

You deserve to learn the Goddess Frame of Mind.

Let's begin, shall we?

<u>*Part One – Learning to Fly*</u>
<u>Chapter One. It All Starts at the Beginning</u>

Greetings and salutations, Goddess, welcome to the Goddess Experience. My step-by-step guide to unlocking the Cosmic Being Within. It is an honor to be sharing my experience with you. You are the reason why I am here, and I appreciate you greatly.

Alright...

So, why am I here?

Well, the very brief overview of it is that about 12-13 years ago, I wanted to die.

YUH...

Never badly enough to actually do it. But, for the *longest* time, I wanted to die.

And when I decided to start really making a difference in the world, I had no idea what I wanted to talk about. In terms of this project being a podcast, an episode a week is quite the task. And, given my zodiac chart - Aries Moon, Gemini Sun, Virgo Rising, I never do anything ½ assed. (I just go full boar with something until I run out of jet fuel and move on to the next project xD)

Initially, I thought this should be about writing. Like, how to be a successful independent author in the modern industry.

Hahahahahahhaha.

I don't know how to be a successful independent author yet!

So, yeah, that wasn't actually a legitimate solution.

But, I do know how to rise up out of a broken heap and into a powerful Goddess (AKA Cosmic Being).

So, that's what I'm here to talk to you about.

Going from pity party to pride parade, and letting your Cosmic wings stretch and unfurl so you can fully fly .

Yes.

But, for today, I'd just like to introduce myself. And, because I'm not just here for me, I'm 110% here for. YOU, I'd love it if you introduced yourself on my forum, at:

I want to know my Cosmic Tribe because I LOVE my Cosmic Tribe!

Don't worry though, I'll go first.

Hi.

My name is Eirian Naomi, or Eiry for short.

I am an author, and long time abuse survivor and self-healer.

I was in an abusive relationship from the time I was 13, until I was 18 years old, which was way more malicious than that sentence sounds.

I realized recently that I essentially grew up like a mole woman, except for I was still roaming around in the world, which was my saving grace.

And it all starts at the beginning.

At 13, I was depressed and drowning in feelings of loneliness. I had been planning on committing suicide the weekend I met my ex, and, at the time it seemed like a gift from Cos.

"Here. Here is a companion for you. You don't have to die. You're not alone."

But I was alone.

I had completely isolated myself.

And, like a frog put on the stove in a pot of cold water before it's brought to a boil, I had no idea I was about to be cooked.

So, the first two years, we fought and fucked and pretended that everything was okay. But, when we realized that the fighting needed to stop, I stopped, and he sure as fuck didn't.

And yet, I still held on for the ride until after I graduated highschool. And then, managed to get out through a series of magical events that occurred because of one simple mindset shift that I made.

I became firm on my belief that I don't need a man to make me happy. Nor do I need a man (or woman) to be successful and take care of myself.

That first mindset shift from distressed damsel to hero-of-my-own-journey was the most important one, because it was the first mindset shift I ever made. And finding that power to believe in myself changed my life forever.

And now, a little over a decade after making that first mindset shift, I am able to talk to you about it now, and hopefully guide you through your own journey so it doesn't take the better half of a decade for you to fully plug into your power!

I write books filled with love and light so that some young girl in a bad situation can stumble upon some hope and turn it into something.

I care about the wounded birds with broken wings who still want to fly.

I wrote this book to remind YOU that you're not alone.

BECAUSE, WHEN I WAS stuck, I stumbled upon a podcast where a goddess was rehashing all of her trauma. It was brutal and raw and made me realize just how lucky I was that my trauma was relatively mild in comparison. It helped me break into my strong demeanor today. It helped birth the Keoni Magnolia Series. And it connected me with a woman who I have never met in person and rarely talk to, but love dearly. She has since taken her podcast down and started her new life as a loving mother and wife, so out of respect for my friend, I won't mention what podcast it was, because you can't find it anymore anyways.

It was my connection with the host, however, that started my Keoni Magnolia project, initially as a series of emails that I sent to my friend because she had shared SO MUCH on her podcast, I had felt the need to pour my heart out and tell her what I had been through.

But I could only get so far. At that time, Keoni was still me and I hadn't learned how to pull fiction out of the facts of my life yet, so it was a very painful road to go down. And to this day, I am still unsure of whether or not I could ever fully rehash the details of what I had went through. It is in the past, and I wake up every day without letting it define me.

The Keoni Magnolia series is about a young girl recovering from her trauma, so I am not going to go into any detail with my own personal story here. That's not why I came here today. We are not here to dread.

We're here to heal and move forward.

Because it doesn't matter **_what_** has happened to us collectively.

It matters that the dark forces of the universe manifested in the physical realm, in one way or another, that severely impacted your life.

It matters that you were hurt.

That you had your power stripped away from you.

That you were left wondering if you are even worthy of the breath you breathe.

IT MATTERS THAT THESE wounds run deep into your soul and can prevent you from achieving your goals and fulfilling your destiny.

IT'S BULLSHIT.

And it's time to do something about it!

It doesn't matter what happened, but that it happened at all, and you don't have to be alone anymore.

You were never truly alone to begin with.

When you take your healing journey into your own hands, you enter into a collective tribe of healers who think about things in terms of their highest and greatest good and harming none. It takes a lot of strength and courage to hold this book in your hands and know that in the end, everything will be okay. That you ARE whole and complete as you are. And that NO ONE is allowed to take your power away from you. Welcome to the mystical band of people who refuse to live in fear of what might happen next. Congratulations on taking your fate into your own hands. I am incredibly proud of you.

And you should be too.

You are such a strong warrior.

A radiant being of love and light.

And you deserve to know that, from the inside out, and through every fiber of your body.

It is my job to help you realize it if you don't already know it, help you remember it when you forget how great you are, and show you how to fully unleash your inner Divine Cosmic Being (Goddess) by sharing my journey from over the better half of a decade to assist you through your journey at an accelerated rate.

We're going to talk about everything from meditation to exercise and eating without the dreaded "D" word (dieting).

Because I am sick and tired of people feeling broken. Feeling like they don't belong anywhere. Feeling like they could never be whole...

Because I KNOW that feeling.

I used to be haunted by it.

I LIVE for being whole, and if I can do it, damn it, SO CAN YOU!!!

Now, before we begin, I do need to add a large disclaimer.

Sis.

Broheim.

As much as I wish I had the divine power to, I cannot get you out of an abusive situation, and neither can this book.

I only know what I did to get out of my situation, and that was to wait until the right time opened up for me to leave. I could have died this way, and do not recommend that method to anyone who is struggling to get out of a dangerous situation.

If you are in an abusive situation, PLEASE get a higher authority involved – the police, or a trustworthy adult if you're still a minor – but please, please, PLEASE do not sit and wait in silence like I did. You're worth more than that and deserve better!

This book is for after the abuse has ended.

Discovering how to return to normal life when you have no idea what normal is anymore. The after care. Learning how to love yourself again. And more importantly, how to trust yourself again.

No one prepared me for the self aftercare.

No one told me that I would be working on myself for the rest of my life.

No one told me about the lasting effects of what I had gone through.

Fuck, I thought that literally the only demographic to experience PTSD was combat soldiers!

NO ONE EVER TOLD ME that I could let this moment, this blip on my timeline, define who I was for the rest of my life, or that I could let it redefine the rest of my life for the better.

No one told me that I could **_choose_**.

I had to figure it all out the hard way.

And it took EIGHT AND A HALF YEARS!

Eight and a half years to understand how to control my internal environment. It was hard, and stressful, and almost cost me my relationship more than once, but I fucking did it.

I made it through to where I feel whole.

I feel juicy.

I feel **_alive_**.

I feel happy, inside and out.

And I finally feel comfortable sitting here talking to you about it.

And I know that I can help you regain control of your own mindset.

There's no shortcut to healing, but hopefully it won't take you the better half of a decade to learn what I've learned. Hopefully, this book will accelerate your healing, as well as your growth. Because you DESERVE it.

You deserve to know in every cell of your being that you are worthy.

You are worthy of everything that you desire.

Worthy of that raise.

Worthy of genuine affection.

Worthy of being your own boss.

Worthy of buying yourself a house.

You are worth so much more than living in the shadow of your past or family history.

You are worthy of living in the bright, beautiful fullness of your present.

You deserve to pull your dreams into reality.

SO, I WANT YOU TO TAKE a moment to ask yourself: *are you a victim, or a warrior?*

Did you fall prey to that... or did you survive that?

Did your trauma define your life, or did it redefine your perspective?

You ARE a warrior.

You ARE a survivor.

And it's time to redefine your perspective.

Because you are worth it.

And I'm here to tell you that you are worth it because I never would have been able to put my faith and trust back into the universe if I'd never heard podcasts that told me that I was worth it.

The universe spoke to me through astrological videos, intuitive channels, internet coaches, and the posts that my friends shared in their stories. And I was bombarded with message after message of stepping into my own power. Without that input, I never would have seen the walls that I had built around myself.

I had told myself that I was broken, repeatedly.

I wanted to be financially stable, but positioned myself as "broke" anytime I spoke about money.

I would blame toxic behaviors on what I had been through, touting those behaviors as unavoidable, instead of taking responsibility for my actions.

In fact, I had shirked my sense of self-responsibility to the point of begging for miracles, rather than taking the initiative to change my situation.

I was desperate.

I was unhappy.

And I felt like I was out of options.

And that was _**AFTER**_ leaving my abusive relationship.

I was creating issues in my own life because deep down, in the pit of my soul, I did not believe that I was worthy of happiness.

YEAH!

Just let that sink in for a minute...

So, anytime my life and relationship was going well, I would sabotage my own happiness!

(If that sounds familiar *at ALL* then you are in the right place.)

I would find things to be overwhelmed by.

And if Pumpkin had a solution to the issue at hand, I would just find infinity more problems because I was overwhelmed by the thought of being happy.

Deep in my subconscious, I believed that I was unworthy of happiness.

And it wasn't until I began consciously working on my worth that I stumbled upon this epiphany.

Keep in mind, this was when I thought that I had really made leaps and bounds with my self-esteem as I had already spent years on my healing journey.

But, it's always really easy to think that you're doing well until you begin actively working on yourself.

And I knew that I needed change.

I knew I needed to switch from scarcity to abundance mindset.

And I knew I needed to own my worth.

And guess what?

Owning your worth means coming face to face with your feelings of unworth.

Mmm-hmm.

Owning your worth means coming face to face with your feelings of unworth.

We're going to be doing a lot of work over the course of this book so that you can learn how to rise up into your full power.

Owning your worth means coming face to face with your feelings of unworth.

Learning to love yourself means addressing the things that you hate about yourself.

Basking in your light means seeing your gremlins first.

It's just facts.

You've got to wade through the shit field before you get to the flower garden.

Shit, you need to pour manure on the field to get the prettiest flowers!

It is time to take your trauma and allow it to fertilize your mental garden instead of suffocate it.

And it's now or never.

Grab a piece of paper and a pen, or open up the notepad on your device, and write down the things you want but feel like you can't achieve.

Don't worry, I'll go first.

I want happiness.

I want financial stability.

I want a healthy and balanced relationship.

I want a career that aligns with my soul's purpose.

I want to succeed at my dreams. (I want to achieve my goals. I want to live out my dreams.)

Simple.

So take a moment, and write your list.
It can be as long, or as short as you need it to be.
What do you want, Sugar Plum?

I want happiness.
I want financial stability.
I want a healthy and balanced relationship.

I want a career that aligns with my soul's purpose.

I want to succeed at my dreams.

What do YOU want?

Okay.

Now that you have your list, I want you to write *another* list. The same list, but instead of the words "I want", write "I am worthy of."
Ready?
Rewrite that list.
I am worthy of happiness.
I am worthy of financial stability.
I am worthy of a healthy and balanced relationship.

I am worthy of a career that aligns with my soul's purpose.
I am worthy of succeeding at my dreams.

Mm-hmm.

Now, say it out loud three to five times in a row to help it seep into your bones.

As a placeholder, I will have you repeat my foundational five affirmations, but as soon as you have YOUR list of what you are worthy of, that is what I want you to speak into being, for your highest and greatest good and harming none. It is the magic of YOUR words, not mine, that really makes this exercise potent and powerful.

I am worthy of happiness.
I am worthy of financial stability.
I am worthy of a healthy and balanced relationship.

I am worthy of a career that aligns with my soul's purpose.
I am worthy of succeeding at my dreams.

Now, how are you feeling?
Glowing?
Like you can take on the world?
I hope so.

If not, we'll get there. It's okay if you need time to learn how to feel worthy of the things that you want. It's okay if you're not capable of fully absorbing the message of this chapter upon the first time that you read it – that's actually how I recognized my own blockages around worth, I would start to tune out when the inspirational videos I was watching would bring up the topic!

It took me a lot of concentrated focus and meditation to fully believe inside and out that I am worthy of happiness, financial stability, a healthy and balanced relationship, and so on.

And I know what it's like to be turned off.

To tune out.

To shift focus to completely avoid confronting the topic of self worth, even when you're by yourself...

But, your healing journey starts today.

You can make the tough decision of learning how to grow through your own personal experience, or you can pretend that you didn't love every minute of this first chapter, and put this book down and find some other way to spend your time. The choice is up to you.

I will love you no matter what your decision.

But... do YOU love YOU?

If you're ready to laugh and cry through the growing pains so that you can spread your wings and fly then give me a *YAAAASSSS QUEEEN!!!!* (yass queen.)

Now, before we go, I want to remind you that *you are loved, you are supported, you are worthy, you are loved, you are supported, you are worthy, you are loved, you are supported, you are worthy.*

From this point forward, you are surrounded by a protective bubble of light, and many blessings shall be ushered forth into your life.

Because you are worthy of happiness.

You are worthy of love,

You are worthy of security.

You are worthy of abundance.

You are worthy of safety.

You are worthy of life.

Thank you, thank you, thank you, and so it is – for your greatest and highest good, and harming none.

Chapter Two. Recovery is a Bitch

So, now that you know that you are worthy of embarking on this journey in the first place, I want to talk to you about the sharp edges on this double sided sword.

In the first chapter of this book, I discussed how my journey began and how "I'm better now," right?

Wrong!

As humans on this planet, we will always be learning and growing and changing. It's not "I'm better now," it's, "I work damn hard to maintain a constantly shifting homeostasis!"

And, as you can tell by the title of this chapter: *recovery is a bitch.*

Recovery is a bitch!

I'm just going to come right out and say it. It's not easy. It's not fucking fun. And it doesn't always feel good.

Recovery is a bitch.

And maybe it's easier for someone who goes into traditional therapy right away, but I wouldn't know because traditional therapy has never made sense to me or been available to me when I needed it most. So, I've rehabilitated myself without medical intervention thus far and that self-rehab is what I'm talking about when I say, "Recovery is a bitch."

But whether you are able to figure things out "on your own" or you have the strength, courage, and resources to go talk to a licensed professional, the sentiment remains the same.

Recovery is a bitch.

Whether you prefer traditional methods or alternative ones, recovery is a bitch because you have got to want it.

You have got to want it.

You need to buckle down and strap in for you and you alone.

No one else can do it for you.

No one else can make you do it if you are not ready.

And let me tell you, **living a healthy, peaceful, non-toxic lifestyle, without the crazymaking and the absurd drama is entirely worth it.**

But, you've got to want it.

You've got to feel the will of the universe coursing through you and crave the reality where you are well. And with addiction recovery, I've heard it repeated over and over and over again, *"you've got to do it for yourself."*

And, yes, that is 100% true.

You can't succeed if you don't want it for yourself.

But for me, and my trauma recovery, the thing that pulled me through from the shadow realm to the sunshine valley was being able to answer the question, *"What do you live **FOR**?"*

What do you live for?

The answer to that question is crucial.

What are your reasons for waking up in the morning, Goddess?

Is it the stars?

The sunrise?

The song of the birds?

The smell of fresh bread?

Snuggles from the dog or cat?

What are your reasons for waking up in the morning?

What makes you excited to be alive, here, on this planet?

I REMEMBER WHEN I BARELY knew the answer to that question.

But then, I remembered that writing had always been my life raft.

And then I remembered that I could be happy and successful without being in a romantic relationship.

... AND THEN I GOT CRAZY lucky and met my twin flame...

Love is now my primary reason to live.

AND I BELIEVE THAT in a healthy relationship, that is a perfectly acceptable answer to that question.

In a codependent situation, it can turn even healthy relationships into toxic ones, but with the right care and respect, *love* is a beautiful reason to live.

And thankfully, "love" isn't just limited to romantic love. There are a gajillion different types of love.

A lot of other Goddesses in my life found that reason to live within supporting a child. It's the same reason why everyone should have some kind of pet that tethers them to a sense of responsibility. And it can also mean your love for cooking, writing, tennis... *ANYTHING*. That is the fascinating part of loving life, when you love yourself, love will come, and you will be so filled with radiant energy that you can't help but love all aspects of your life, or at least figure out how to change your circumstances so that you CAN.

IF YOU DON'T KNOW ME, I'm a romantic. My healthy relationship gave me a reason to live, and a reason to better myself. I know that it is an incredible privilege to have found another human being worthy of my being because he helped me see my deep inner worth.

Of course I believe in the power of love, but that's just me. The thing about love is that you've got to give love to receive love. But the love that you need to give, is to *yourself.*

It's a hard pill to swallow, but you need to love yourself before love will ever be capable of loving another.

No matter how badly you want it, if you don't first love yourself, all of your actions are based out of hate. And it's silly to think you can make wise decisions about life when you hate yourself.

It was one of the hardest concepts for me to grasp, but it sounds as obvious as a fucking mountain range when I write it down here for you now.

When you love yourself, love will come.

The hard part of recovery is remembering what self-love is. Eradicating the self-deprecating humor, recognizing negative statements, dropping sarcasm, and being positive of yourself instead of critical.

Did you know that criticism can be really damning? Not criticism with the intent of betterment, but the hyper-critiques of any perfectionist are not healthy. And depending on what you've been through, you may have had that "useful" perfectionism branded into your personality with a red hot cattle iron.

Recovery is hard.

However many years your toxic and traumatic experiences lasted just makes the recovery period take longer, because you have to unlearn the toxic behaviors and relearn the healthy ones.

And that process can hurt, a lot.

That process is the reason why I wish I could've gotten into therapy a lot earlier in my journey. Because I had no idea what a healthy relationship was. And, maybe if I'd had an objective guide to show me what healthy behaviors are, I wouldn't have spent eight and half years figuring out how to heal. *BUT* it is what it is, and I just fumbled my way through our relationship until I started causing drama in my healthy relationship; because all I had ever known in my life was toxic behavior.

Yet, Pumpkin was unbelievably patient with me, that I was allowed several opportunities to learn new healthy patterns.

So far, I feel like this sounds like a canine obedience training course, so I will give you a more relatable story.

AT THE BEGINNING OF my recovery, I was taking Pumpkin dinner at work. And when I got out of the car, I dropped the bowl of food that I had brought, shattering the bowl and ruining dinner completely.

I was overwhelmed with disappointment and guilt. I began sobbing, feeling stupid and incompetent as all the emotions that had been literally beaten into me in my previous... ahem... lifetime came flooding back to me. I had just begun doing some minimal soul work on myself, so I at least understood the reaction, but it was so bad that my entire being was shaking with the stored trauma of my past.

Needless to say, it ruined my whole night.

Recently... well, okay, back in 2020, I had a similar experience. I was at home, had just finished cooking, and was getting ready to take a big bowl of food to the other room. My hand slipped and the bowl of food shattered on the hardwood floor.

I was sent spiraling into a flashback of the aforementioned night, and any night of my childhood where dishes were broken in one fight or another.

And it shook me.

I was down for a good 15 minutes.

It was the exact same feeling as I had had that night in 2012 and I just let the tears fall, releasing the trauma, releasing the hurt, and releasing the pain, in the safe, warm kitchen of our apartment, over 100 miles away from where we had grown up... over 100 miles away from where I had been tormented.

And I let it go.

Released it back to the universe.

After years of studying, and finally knowing how to heal.

RECOVERY IS A BITCH.

I've never been diagnosed with PTSD, but I do feel comfortable claiming it.

What I went through *should* produce PTSD.

Trauma over an extended period of time causes PTSD. PERIOD.

And I believe that a lot of us can go on living our lives in extreme denial until something major throws us back into reality and we react.

For me, it was seeing my ex as a customer at my gas station (back when we had first broken up). I had a panic attack at the mere sight of his car.

That's when I realized I had a problem.

SO, I DID A LOT OF journaling to get the toxicity out of my spirit, and managed to avoid therapy by partying and casually conversing about what I'd gone through like it was nothing.

I had no idea that telling all of my close coworkers over the years was largely therapeutic! I thought I just enjoyed having my freedom again!!

I've always been a talker. But when I began researching PTSD to bring awareness to it, I came across articles mentioning that not talking about your trauma is one of the biggest avoidance techniques out there, because when you don't talk about it, you don't even acknowledge that your trauma exists!

To me, that in and of itself, is a form of giving away your personal power. Because you can't control your reaction to something you deny is real.

Let that sink in.

To heal, you must first admit that you have wounds.

IT MAY BE A HARD PILL to swallow...

But, recovery is a bitch.

RECOVERY IS A BITCH because you don't always know what will bring on a flashback, or trigger you. It's not always the same thing, or consistent, either. And as you take care of old triggers, new ones will come up, and that's not something I was prepared for. Because I didn't do my research (since I had limited resources for doing so) and I thought that trauma was just one gigantic thing to deal with all at once.

But what I learned is that it's like a three tiered cake – you need people to help you eat it, and you've got to eat all of it, so at some point, it's going to make you sick. And THEN, you're the one who has to take all the leftovers home and the only way to clear up space in your freezer is by eating the damn thing!

That's why recovery is a bitch.

And it's not like it's your favorite cake either. Sure, maybe the outer layers are the most enticing cake you can think of, but the more you eat, you realize there's different flavors hidden in there, like Bertie Bott's Every Flavored Bean flavors – dirt, earthworms, burnt hair, and vomit – hidden within the layers of red velvet and mint chocolate chip. But you still have to eat all of it.

Ugh.

And the only way it really truly works is by having a solid support system.

I got really lucky. My partner – Pumpkin – provided (and still provides) a <u>galaxy</u> of support, even when shit was really hard and my recovery was breaking our relationship down to the foundation so that we could build a better, more stable house. And wow, does it <u>hurt!</u>

If there's only one thing you take away from this chapter, let it be that recovery is <u>NOT</u> easy.

THE ONLY REASON I MENTION it is because **I** thought that it was going to be easy, so I was lax on putting in the work, and then it took me eight and a half years to fully let go of it.

Eight and a half years, and I still have triggers! But at least now I know how to deal with them.

And dealing with them can be a bitch somedays too. I went three or four years before the mall became one of my triggers.

I didn't like malls in general after I was out of high school and thought that it was just personal growth rather than avoidance. The consumerism lifestyle didn't suit me anymore, and if I was going to be immersed in a large crowd of people, I'd prefer being at an EDM concert or festival.

It really didn't seem like avoidance at all. It just felt like a natural part of growing up.

But then, we bought a coat online that didn't fit and needed to go return it in person.

As soon as my foot hit the parking lot pavement, I was overwhelmed with anxiety and flashback after flashback after flashback. The mall had been our old stomping ground when I was in high school because our hometown really lacked anything else to do. The mall provided shopping, food, and entertainment, all in one place! And I hadn't realized how much time I had spent there during my abusive relationship until that very moment, years later.

Thankfully, I had been doing research on PTSD recovery at that time and knew that going in and confronting the anxiety would be way more beneficial to me than ignoring it and going back to the car while Pumpkin returned that Cos-Blessed coat.

It did make me a stronger person...

But, fuck was it uncomfortable! And it didn't fix it right away either. We'd go to the mall on occasion after that, to patronize GameStop, and for a while, those trips would trigger me too.

And all I could do was breathe deeply while perusing the video games. Sometimes Pumpkin would grab hold of my hand or encapsulate me in a hug from behind to ground me in my current reality.

Because studies show that your brain doesn't know the difference between past, present, future, and dreamland. If you dream about doing something, you'll improve that skill and the next time you do it in real life, you'll be better at it.

On the other end of that super fascinating spectrum, your brain also doesn't know the difference between now and then. So, when you smell something, hear something like a name or a song, see something, or enter certain buildings/neighborhoods, your brain goes back to "then".

I never knew this until I began researching trauma so that I could help others move past it the way I have. And this anomaly within the human mind is actually why flashbacks in and of themselves are traumatic and incredibly invasive.

I've had flashbacks stop me in my tracks and completely consume me. It can ruin your day, and it can happen at random. The only one that I could really expect was when I was having intimacy issues and was triggered by kisses when Pumpkin's beard was too long.

Those flashbacks were also the worst because Pumpkin and I have always had a very strong intimate connection and when I was having those issues, he'd kiss me and then his beard would shoot me reeling back into icky, slimy memories. And it was heartbreaking because I _had_ to pull away and ask him to shave immediately. That was torture. And I think that most of the other sporadic flashbacks didn't really start until after I'd healed my beard-wound.

And I got _really_ lucky to have a pumpkin that I can trust, who gave me a reason to <u>want</u> to resolve the issue AND who respected the fact that it was a legitimate issue.

That respect thing is key when it comes to the success of your support system. And I can't say entirely how long it took me to work through the main big trigger(s). I don't remember, honestly, because we have a healthy connection and I didn't think about it until I was triggered.

Eventually, the beard triggers got fewer and farther between and I'm sure there was a point when I noticed that his full beard wasn't setting me off anymore, and thanked the cosmos.

But, because there were so many other triggers to follow after I'd healed that single issue, I never saved the date. And for me, personally, my flashbacks would catch me off guard.

For the most part, it was the days or moments when I'd be zipping along thinking I was doing phenomenally well in my recovery that something random and unexpected would set me off.

And I used to take those moments super personally too. Used to think that because I was still susceptible to having flashbacks that I was sucking balls at healing my past wounds. But, I see it the complete opposite way now.

I've recently found that those triggers and how you respond to them are monuments to your success. In the beginning, those moments are hard. Like, <u>*REALLY*</u>, extraordinarily hard. But then, you realize it was just a memory. A reminder from the universe to keep getting better and to continue gaining control over the ghosts that still haunt you.

When you fully connect yourself to your inner Goddess, you will find these moments strengthening your soul. Even when they break you down, it is only to build you back up.

Recovery is a bitch.

Just like working out to get that thicc, juicy, peach emoji beach bohdi, it hurts, it makes you sweat, and even makes you cry. There are no shortcuts other than arming yourself with information, and it is *fully* worth it.

Whether it's right now, or as you find time this week, I want you to grab a pen and a notebook and make a list of your known triggers. (And if you haven't already, you should definitely dedicate a notebook to your own Goddess Experience!)

Write down your known triggers. What gives you anxiety? What gives you flashbacks?

Don't worry, I'll go first.

Most of these triggers are things I've worked past, but I've been on this healing journey for a decade as of typing this book. Your list will be longer or shorter depending on where you are on your own journey.

My known triggers have been:

- Beards past a certain length.

- Blue eyed, blonde dudes

- Certain, very specific songs

- Hearing my ex's name (super fucking common name. 10 years later it still kind of bugs me, but I'm mostly used to it.)

- Certain parts of my hometown (neighborhoods)

- Tense situations

- Public conflict between others (like a couple fighting in a parking lot, or a child throwing a tantrum.)

- Certain TV shows.

- Certain movies.

- The mall in my hometown

- Seeing my ex's truck (not the general make and model, but specifically his vehicle and I only got over this after moving 100 miles away from my hometown and finding out that my ex lives where I moved to. Lolololol. Small ass world.)

So, what's your list, Goddess?

Once you've identified your list, it'll be easier for you to address your trauma.

And why do you want to address your trauma, Goddess?

Because you are fucking WORTH IT!!!!!

Chapter Three. It Gets Better

There **is** a light at the end of this tunnel. If you work hard and stay self-aware, you **can** move forward and into a better life. You are worth the effort of grueling work to see massive change in your life for your greatest and highest good and harming none.

You should be incredibly proud of yourself for being here after reading the last chapter. You could have run away screaming and donated this book to the library or dropped it off at your nearest Little Free Library and never looked back. But you are still here, because you take your healing seriously, and you know that the payoff will be worth the effort.

I applaud you.

It takes strength. Courage. Passion. Bravery. And dedication to **want** to change and then **act** upon that desire. So, I am going to take a minute to give you a round of applause and encourage you to give yourself a pat on the back.

Well done, Goddess! Well done!

Okay! Now, before I dive in, I want to make sure you have your trusty notebook and magick pen, because I <u>will</u> have a new exercise for you at the end of this chapter, and I wanted to give you a heads up this time (in case you weren't expecting that at this point).

So...

Recovery is a bitch.

A painful, fickle bitch, which takes you and breaks you down so that you can rise, like a phoenix from the ashes, a stronger, better, renewed version of yourself. And it is that mystical experience of rising from the ashes of your former self is what makes it worth it.

And...

This chapter was hard to craft because I want to sit here and state "you" statements.

<u>*You'll*</u> feel this and <u>*you'll*</u> feel that.

But, the reality of those statements is that I genuinely don't know how you'll feel about your recovery, and I'm okay admitting that and being transparent with you.

The only person I have ever guided through this type of recovery has been myself, and under a very special set of circumstances that worked out well for me, but, which I would also never wish upon anyone.

However, it is my **favorite** story, because the ending is a pretty fantastic one, and the next story book in my series has been phenomenal!

What I can recommend is training your mind to **enjoy** being healthy, and that's why I'm here writing this book for you to hold in your hands, to teach you to train your mind to reconnect your logic to your intuition, and to get you into a positive headspace, because that is what worked for me.

So, it starts with finding the reason for waking in the morning. Finding the reason to change and then pursuing the change. And the change is hard and painful.

But, remember, it gets better.

I found in my journey that the more I could handle the tender, raw moments with a level head, the more proud and sure enough I could become. And it's the little things.

At first it was significantly shortening the duration of my episodes by being conscious of my behaviors, making a note of my patterns and distracting myself sooner so I wouldn't get sucked into obsessing over negativity. And because of that, my episodes are nearly avoidable all together.

When I first escaped the madness, I didn't think that I was pretty. I couldn't look myself in the eye for over a year after my trauma ended. And it wasn't due to a lack of love on Pumpkin's part. In fact, I stopped wearing makeup because I knew that he was being honest when he told me that I was beautiful.

(Did I mention that I'm a Happily Ever After New-Adult Fiction author?)

But I didn't love myself as much as I thought I did, and I had quite a bit of shit to work on. And it was _hard_ but day by day, I got more comfortable looking at myself in the mirror again. And day by day, things that I hated about myself started to become things I loved about myself. Slowly, I got more and more beautiful. And I was able to truly value my existence because I feel like if one extra little thing had gone wrong, or been slightly more intense, I could have died. In addition to _wanting_ to die, my abusive relationship was so dangerous that if it was a couple of degrees further into the red zone, my ex could have killed me.

And once you see the beauty in life, it really makes you want to live it.

And in order to heal yourself, you must give to yourself. Hold space for yourself. Make time for the things that you love and the things that you want to explore. Feed yourself knowledge and positive vibes from many trusted sources. Because to heal to the point of forgiveness, release, and retribution is one of the most magickal things to do.

And I know that if _I_ can do it, _anyone_ is capable of doing it.

Because we are _all_ Goddesses. And Goddesses create the reality that they want to live in.

I'll let that sink in for a moment.

Goddesses create the reality they want to live in.

So, you can either continue to feel broken, destitute, poor, and whatever other poisonous bullshit you have been fed. Or, you can exorcise those demons and create the reality in which you are healthy with well balanced, meaningful relationships, and a fulfilling life.

Considering that you are here, I really hope that you're looking forward to creating your new existence.

If not, I encourage you to put this book down now and give it to a friend. This is not for you if you are not intending to radically change your life.

NOW, AS A CULTIVATOR and facilitator of Goddesses, I must say that in my personal experience, every milestone fuels you to the next one. So, after that first breakthrough, everything is easier, and then you have another breakthrough, and another, and another, and after so many incredibly breakthroughs, it gets easier and easier to have faith in yourself and trust that you will make it through the triggers and flashbacks next time. Trust that you have the ability to make good decisions. Believe that you learned from your lessons, and that you can grow from them.

The juicy fruits of your labor.

The diamonds in the deep levels of the mines.

The reward that you worked so hard to achieve.

It gets better, it really does.

For me personally, my recovery has been like climbing a mountain that looks short, but is truly very steep and daunting. There were many times where I gelt like I was at the top, but then you look past the trees and realize that there's still miles of mountain to climb.

And there were also times when I completely wanted to give up. Stay plateaued and just deal with it.

But the real reward comes in finishing the climb. Being able to look back at what you accomplished with a crystal clear, bird's eye view – completely on a new wavelength and elevation.

I promise you, it gets better.

One thing that will always stand out to me is that I used to be chunky (which is why I still want to be thicc) and I couldn't run very fast or climb stairs without being winded, and really it was less my weight, and more what I was eating (which we'll dive into next chapter) and I was told that I could never walk several miles – that I was too fat and lazy.

Fast forward nearly a decade and Pumpkin and I love going for hikes and literally climbing mountains.

That's beautiful to me.

The fact that I literally proved my ex-boyfriend's toxic view of me wrong. Even though my ex may _never_ know about that. It's not really for him to know.

The only thing that matters in that equation is that I know that I've overcome my past reality.

And that's not even something that I intended to do. Despite any poisonous communication, I actually love fitness, and always have, ever since I was little. There was just a point in my life when the darkness of the universe wanted to stamp out my light, and I had to prove that my light was worth shining.

I'm going to do something a little different for this chapter and share a poem with you about my creative journey. I feel like it directly shows just exactly how it gets better.

<u>Finding Myself</u>
<u>(What 2020 Taught Me)</u>
I've always been a writer
Literally
I started writing as soon as I could hold a pen
Divinely inspired with genuine passion
So Santa brought me a table to write at for my third Christmas
I've always been a writer.
But somehow, you come to this planet with a strong
Conviction for who you are and the devil can still
Come along to shake that up
To instill doubt
To tell you that you don't know any better
And that your dreams are stupid
And you're worth nothing
But the devil is a liar
An none of these whispered thoughts are true
And you have to learn to work past them
So I came to this planet knowing myself
And then life got weird and I got lost
Thinking that nothing would come of this hobby
Nobody reads
J.K Rowling was a fluke, a glitch in the system
"If you really want to make your money writing,
You need to make it first and then retire to write,"
All evil hisses
The whispers in my ear telling me I would amount to
Nothing
Yet, I knew deep down that it wasn't true
Wasn't true
Even if I didn't know exactly what I would do
I knew I possess the power to be with the moon

Immortalized by the sun
Cherished by everyone
And I found myself blocked from writing
From really creating anything substantial
Upon graduating high school, I
Found myself
In love
(For real this time!)
And I
Found myself
Wanting to party
And I
Found myself
Wanting to forget
And heal
And recover
And I
Found myself
Wanting to experience new things
I was able to go back and enhance and fall in love
With a Cinderella short I'd written in school
Because we were going to shows
Living in the moment
And existing as modern-day, stationary gypsies
I quit tobacco
I quit make-up
I quit my bra
I dreaded my hair and then, I
Found myself
Regretting that.
And
Afraid of shaving my head, I ripped them apart

And then cut my hair to my ears
(Fucking, Ouch) (And I'd later shave my head... twice!)
And I published my first book, only to later discover
It was technically unfinished, and would later be
Edited, twice, before becoming a complete novel.
And I waited,
And I
Found myself disappointed that my zombie novella
Didn't net 10g's in the first 10 weeks, and I
Found myself giving up.
"Writing isn't going to make me money"
"Well, it was worth a try, guess I'll do something else..."
And I did
I started crocheting,
Which I didn't think would lead to anything, initially
I just wanted to make Pumpkin a set of juggling balls for a music
festival.
And then I made myself a shawl... and shorts...
And a top.
And then one of our friends found out about my skill and I
Found myself crocheting her a pair of legwarmers
In trade for a custom hat.
And then I
Found myself thinking I was set
I could crochet or a side hustle, make enough to retire
And then, I could spend my days writing

But then I
Found myself missing writing,
Every time I sat down with yarn and hook I pinned to be
Sitting with pen and book, plume and ink, just words and me.

But that's not where everyone's making their money!
Besides, when's the last time you had an idea, honey?
Thinkin' this is how you'll do it is mighty funny!
That evil voice would hiss in my ear, having been
Spoken by mentors, and spoken by peers
Breaking me down, causing me tears
Getting me to chase my tail for years and years
Causing me to live in the shadow of my fears.
Lost
So I
Found myself putting crochet on the back burner
To try becoming a hula-hoop instructor
I took the eight-week course, got my certificate
And choked.
Sure, I was young, and tbh, my intentions were
...misaligned
So I found myself
Having spent a fair amount of money and time
On something that I decided to never use.
I found myself
Missing writing, so I turned back to crochet,
Because that makes sense, right?
It did turn out "so well" the first time
eye roll face palm
That's your twenties for you (winkie face)
I started a GoFundMe
I had big dreams and big goals
I was going to raise the money to start crocheting
Full-time and then once I was at that point, I would
Write,
Right...?
Definitely sound logic.

But the funds didn't come.
I have a beautiful tote filled with yarn from
My fairy grandmother
But the universe had other plans
And I was lost. I
Found myself writing in the in-between
And I found that I was in love
In love with creating intricate worlds to get lost in
And share
But for years I had convinced myself that it simply
Couldn't be done. Simply because
Pop stars are actors and musicians
I had built a reality for myself where writing was not
Viable or profitable or a good use of time.
Oh what a sad and limiting existence for a writer to live in!
But I was convinced…

And I found myself
Deciding I would be a rapper
Just like Nicki and Iggy and Cardi
I can write. I'm a girl. All I had to do was do it…
Right?
The year before the virus, the universe called me out.
Sent me a challenge to this dream that I could be a
Cartoon on youtube and entirely circumvent performing.
Oh, delicious delicious twenties. Young and dumb.
Young and dumb.
I found myself in the midst of someone active in
The local music scene.
He encouraged me to go to the open mic nights
At the Tea House

If it had been a bar, I would have said no.
But I went to two.
With my best workplace friend by my side
And never having opened my eyes
During each performance.
The first was a mess. I choked. I mean, it was my first time.
And then, the second night,
A month later
The tea house was packed, people were standing
Shoulder to shoulder (ah, the pre-pandemic vibe)
They had talked through the guest artist's set.
He did this for a living. I was expecting the same amount of respect.
Then it was time for the open mic. My name was
second on the list
But the first name was absent when called so I
Found myself going first. Sparkling with sequins
Shaking with nerves.
And I captivated the audience for two songs
Without music
Just my quivering pink energy, naked and vulnerable
On that stage, pouring my heart out in a
Doors cover and an original rap about
Ultimate Smash Bros
(entitled Ultimately Smashing, and I'm still proud of that shit...
"Feelin' so fly like Kirby, little pink amoeba so no one can hurt me...
constantly
Adapting to my surroundings, I'm ultimately smashing
No one can take that away from me, if you try
I'll kick you off the map, remindin who's truly king,
So smashing, yeah, yeah, so smashing...)
They didn't cheer until I was done, and the whole
Tea house shook with the applause of 30-50 people

(my eyes were closed, so I didn't take count)
And then I moved to a rural town with
One gas station, one grocery store, and no music scene.
If I wanted to go to open mics, I would have to
Organize them myself or drive 45 miles into
The city.
And that's when I realized that I wasn't a performer
I didn't want to tour and play gigs… I wanted to write.
I found myself.
Finally.
And upon having the epiphany that I'm happiest writing
I realized that I also deserve a 9-5
I truly love
And I found a good job at an amazing company
Moved back to the city and rented a room in one of the
Nicest neighborhoods…
It turns out that I had been holding myself back significantly.
December 2019.
Corona corona corona
What could there be to fear about a virus named after a beer
Hahahahaha. It'll never show up here.

In January of 2020, people started getting sick.
This shit was real now. And as the numbers trickled in
So did the anxiety, at first "if", and then "when" they
Would shut it all down.
And then I got sick. It was gnarly. For a week. For a month
I was scared. I never get sick. It made me realize
My mortality. Fuck… 2020 man.
I can't say what it was, gnarled sinus infection or

Walking pneumonia my guesses (although I'll never know, never got
tested)
After a week, when I was well enough to go back to work
I got put on furlough.
You don't have to go home, but you can't stay here kid.
It was the end of March, and the universe gave me
April to work on my craft. My passion. My flame.
But what I ended up doing was Instagramming, procrastinating
And walking the dog a lot.
I thought I got a fair bit one, but I could have done better
And when I got that call that I could go back to work
I cried.
I wept.
I found myself wanting to give up completely.
Overwhelmed at the thought of working 40 hours and
Maintaining the progress I had achieved during my break...
And it wasn't until that moment that I truly
Found myself.

After eight years of agonizing over this predicament
It FINALLY sank in that you've got to do
The thing you love and
You can never give up on yourself.
So I went to work, and continue building my empire.
Juggling my work schedule with my commitment to
My craft and my community.
Sitting hunched in the car in the cold dead of
Morning with my laptop when we moved again and only
Had internet access at the public library.
After 8 years, I finally learned to chase
The dream because of your passion, not the money.

Thanks 2020. It's been real. And I will never be the same.

NOW, I EXPLICITLY IMPLORE you to believe that it gets **better. Because it does. Especially if you believe it will.**

Now, it's your turn to do the work, Goddess.

Think about each of these questions thoroughly and then write the answers down in the notebook that you have dedicated to this process.

Take all the time you need.

This is important, Goddess, it deserves your full attention.

What do you want to heal?

Mmm...

What do you want to heal?

I WANTED TO HEAL FOR an overall better quality of life.

That's probably what it'll boil down to for you as well, but...

What do you want to heal?

Okay, next question.

What is standing in your way?

Mm...

Yes. *What is standing in your way?*

It's time to unearth some of those feelings of ennui and worthlessness.

So...

What's standing in your way?

For me, it was my feelings of worthlessness and overall negative behavior. I felt as though I didn't deserve to be whole, so I would self-sabotage my progress when I noticed that I was making leaps and bounds. And it took years of self-illumination for me to realize that. But, it all boils down to fear and a sense of lack.

What's standing in your way?

Got it?

Good!

Next, I want you to look at those two answers. I have a feeling that regardless of what you wrote down, it is something to do with fear and lack, so I want you to repeat these affirmations out loud:

My journey is beautiful, meaningful, and unique.

I am special, powerful, and confident.

I release my past trauma to the universe.

I allow the universe to absorb my pain so that I may be whole.

I release all feelings of lack.

I radiate divine riches.

I am divine riches.

I allow myself to heal.

Because I am worth it.

I deserve it.

And it gets better.

For the sake of my potential, I forgive my past and promise myself that I deserve to get better for it.

Thank you, thank you, thank you, and so it is.

THANK YOU FOR SPENDING time with me today, Goddess. I am proud of the work that you have done on yourself during this session. I hope you are radiant and glowing, feeling hopeful about the future.

I know that I am hopeful for the future for you.

<u>Chapter Four - The Power of What you Eat</u>

So, now that we've discussed how this journey may challenge you, as well as how it will reward you, it is time to discuss the foundational basics of being a Goddess.

There are three basics that make up the divine trinity, and those are:

1. Mindset/Meditation
2. Food
3. Exercise

In this chapter we are going to discuss Food.

Why are we starting with food when it is the second foundational pillar to being a Goddess?

I don't have a good explanation for that.

But I do have a good story...

Food is where I started with my journey.

I guess that's actually pretty plain and simple, but it does get a little bit more complicated than that.

I was a fast food addict in my teens. Like, ***<u>BAD</u>***. And it got to a point where I'd be walking out the door to go hang out with friends and my beautiful mother would offer me food she'd lovingly made... and I would tell her that I wasn't hungry, and then immediately go eat fast food.

I'd sneak whole meals on my way home, and hide the leftovers in my closet. Eat my mother's home cooked meals, and then finish my leftover closet-food afterwards!

I was drowning my sorrows in food, and it felt easy to justify because food is "good for you."

But not **ALL** food is good for you!

Of course, you do need to take that with a grain of salt because eating something is better than not eating anything at all.

For me, it started because I didn't want to eat cafeteria food anymore. Being in highschool meant being able to go off campus for lunch, and my highschool was practically surrounded by fast food restaurants on all sides.

I thought that, because it wasn't served in a conveyor belt buffet line of food, that I was making healthier choices. *(Later in life, I learned that it all pretty much comes from the same place. Even gas stations and jails... pretty much **anywhere** that serves convenient, ready made foods uses the same supplier, and that completely destroyed my childhood nostalgia around taco salad bowls and pizza sticks.)*

So, I ate out every single day.

I was working and not paying any bills, so I spent the spare money I had on clothes and shitty food. (9 times out of 10, it was on shitty food though.)

I thought that healthy was *Subway, Arby's,* and *Wendy's* (in that order). And I put zero thought into the actual ingredients and source of the food that I was eating.

You know the adage, "You are what you eat?"

Well, let me just say that I had a "fast food physique" – greasy, bloated, and unhealthy. I worked out and managed to chisel out a "bombshell" figure regardless, but one look at me and any seasoned Goddess would have known that I ate more fast food than well thought out meals.

And I was in a toxic relationship, drowning the pain in toxic food, and then, at my lowest point, popping toxic amounts of NSAIDs to numb the pain that wasn't being touched by the bad food (and secret love affairs).

And these toxic habits had some fairly adverse side effects over time.

For me personally, I fucked up my digestion and metabolism. And in the end it wasn't JUST my food affecting that (but we'll talk more about the other stuff in later chapters.)

Food was my starting point for my recovery.

Pumpkin taught me about *Gut and Psychology Syndrome* shortly after we met. One of his roommates had a life threatening journey with food, and learning about GAPS had saved their life.

Initially, GAPS was discovered by Natasha Campbell-McBride. Since then, her teaching has been picked up by many, including Dr. Axe, author of *Eat Dirt*.

Dr. Campbell-McBride's studies have finally linked the correlation between what we eat and what we think. Going so far as to attribute mental illness to bad dietary habits.

I had to listen to her lectures *several* times before absorbing the information and wanting to act upon it.

I used to think it was because of her gorgeous accent, but I'm willing to admit that I had a **LOT** of blockages around food, especially at that time. It's hard to take everything you've ever known about how to survive, completely unlearn it, and then relearn entirely new information.

But, I was hooked. Addiction and mental illness run deep on both sides of my family and here was this doctor declaring that things like bipolar and schizophrenia can be contained by eating better.

Holy shit.

So why?

Why is that?

Well... it's complicated.

Simply put, within the last century or so, we've transitioned from eating simple, natural foods, to eating very complex foods, sometimes even created in a lab. Our bodies were not made in a lab, our bodies were designed by nature. So, we've been eating all this... *stuff* that we weren't designed to digest, and it wears on our health.

Specifically, over time, these harsh foods create small **holes** in your gut.

Fucking terrifying, right?

THESE MICRO-LESIONS allow small particles of food to enter your bloodstream **undigested**, which causes all sorts of problems ranging from physical symptoms such as hives or digestional health, to mental symptoms like brain fog, depression, anxiety, all the way up to **auditory and visual hallucinations** or "episodes" in people who are predisposed to, or diagnosed with, heavier mental health issues.

DAMN.

SO...

Our society has been trained to believe that mental health issues are out of our hands. That we're at the whim of some invisible puppet master, but in reality, <u>we</u> are that puppet master.

Not only that, but Dr. Campbell-McBride makes the point of mentioning that people with addiction issues are trying to self-medicate the mental issues caused by their leaky gut.

I learned this when I was in my golden partying age. Young, dumb, and in love with the rave scene (which was really the "festival" scene that was born out of the rave scene once I got to it.) I loved drinking. I loved partying. I loved being free and forgetting my past.

But **<u>FORGETTING</u>** your past and ***<u>FORGIVING</u>*** your past are two totally different cards in the same deck, and I was still learning that.

(I was 18 and just a baby.)

And because Pumpkin was a legitimate positive force in my life, I realized that I needed to take a hold of the wheel with both hands because it was worth it to have the best quality of life possible.

I want mental stability for myself.

I want a strong, healthy romantic partnership.

I want healthy workplace and personal relationships.

I want to be defined by how I take control of my circumstances, and not by falling victim *to* my circumstances.

THAT is why what you eat is important.

When you step up to the plate and take responsibility for what you're putting in your body, you'll be empowered by the choices you make. Even when you *do* eat out, because let's be honest, sometimes you just want someone else to cook for you without having to do the dishes afterwards, you'll be empowered by that decision.

When you take responsibility for what you eat, you take control of your mental and physical wellbeing.

I will repeat that to let it sink in.

When you take responsibility for what you eat, you take control of your mental and physical wellbeing.

THAT is what being a Goddess is all about.

Taking control of your mental and physical wellbeing.

Because when you take control of your mental and physical wellbeing, you unlock the power within you to create your own reality.

Stop waiting for things to "get better" and start MAKING them better by changing your energy in order to create new opportunities within your own life.

Life is a game.

There are many ways to play it.

And one of the key factors in the trajectory of that game is how we fuel our beings.

In the back of this book, you will find links to the GAPS resources so that you can learn more about how to take control of your overall well being. Dr. Campbell-McBride even has recipes on her website. It is definitely worth checking out.

BEFORE I WRAP UP THIS chapter, I want to share one more story with you.

Pumpkin and I have been together for a decade and then some (at the time of me writing this), and six years into our journey, I had changed everything about my diet, except for cutting out wheat.

I was steadfast in my belief that, because it was whole wheat, it wasn't bothering me.

But it was.

Pumpkin and I began fighting. A lot. Because my comprehension was out the window. I was experiencing brain fog on extreme levels. You could have pointed at a stop sign and told me, "that top sign is red," and I wouldn't have understood what you meant.

We almost broke up.

After 6 beautiful years of intense, deep, healthy love, we almost called it quits in a moment of extreme distress, and I finally put the two and two together that we'd been eating excessive amounts of flour, and that <u>might</u> have been the culprit.

I asked for a week.

One week to prove that it was an external source crossing my wires and not something fundamentally wrong with our relationship. If cutting out bread <u>*didn't*</u> change anything, *then* we'd part ways, because healthy relationships need to recognize toxic behaviors and then change them. And if change can't be applied, then the relationship itself is likely toxic.

To my relief, it was the bread.

And I learned later, or *re*learned I suppose, that this kind of dramatic reaction to food is very common in people with leaky gut. Especially if you're Autistic.

Holy shit.

IT WAS THE MOST FRUSTRATING moment in my life, coming up against severe communication blocks. I can't *imagine* what those symptoms are like for someone with severe Autism!

And it's because gluten is difficult to digest.

So, if you have leaky gut, the gluten can slip into your bloodstream as a peptide, which still needs to be broken down into a protein to be of any use to your body at all, and travels to your brain to cause a temporary ruckus.

I stopped eating wheat for about 2 and a half years, and only tried it again after moving towns. It's enjoyable, but I still have issues if I eat it excessively, and I'm not *addicted* to it the way I used to be.

When I was a kid, I could live off of bread, and now I know that I need to be careful with it.

In addition to wheat, I have an aversion to soy, and intermittent issues with almonds. I choose to avoid processed soy all-together because it causes my body to tremble and that's really unpleasant. I prefer almond flour to wheat flour, but can't eat almond flour everyday without causing issues.

It's all about having the knowledge and awareness to observe those things.

What you eat is super important.

It's time you take advantage of that.

Get out your notebook, Goddess. It's time to take an audit of your time.

THINK BACK TO LAST week.

How many packaged foods did you eat – chips, breakfast bars, cup noodles, etc.

How many times did you eat out?

Was it fast food or expensive dining?

How many meals did you make at home?

If it was out of a box, that counts as packaged foods. If it was a meal made with whole ingredients, it counts here.

Okay?

How many packaged foods or meals did you eat (roughly)?

How many times did you eat out?

And How many meals did you prepare at home/from scratch?

NOW...

How have you felt the last week?

Emotionally, physically, mentally.

Really sit with this for a moment...

How have you felt this last week?

How have you felt this last week?

OKAY.

Now, keep these numbers in mind. This isn't about good or bad. It's just about awareness.

The important thing is that you've been eating. Period.

And I'm proud of you for fueling your cosmic vessel.

FOR ME PERSONALLY, eating more or less processed foods, including take out, has a direct correlation to my mood, physical health, and so on. I make as much food at home as possible. Probably about 80% of my meals are made at home/from scratch. I'm working on eating enough food, while eating at home, and it really is a goal of mine to be eating 100% home cooked meals and snacks, but it's also really tricky while working full-time, so it's always a matter of being gentle with oneself.

Because cooking at home is EXHAUSTING at times.

So, here's what I want you to do.

Take a step back and look at your schedule.

Figure out when you have the most free time in the next 7 days, and pick a day to cook a meal with whole foods. I recommend lunch or dinner.

Pick out a recipe that's just basic ingredients – veggies, meat, beans, rice (WHOLE foods) – and make sure you pick something that sounds amazing. Then, get the ingredients (bonus points if you're able to base a recipe off of what you already have at home!)

I personally love making one pot meals. But I also just love finding new recipes and learning new ways to prepare food.

Begin to build a routine around more thoughtful eating. The more you do it, the easier it will be.

Because, when you take responsibility for your mental health and wellbeing, you take control of your life.

Chapter Five - The Power of What You Think (Part One)

In the last chapter we discussed how what you eat and the health of your gut are of the utmost importance when it comes to maintaining your mental health. But life isn't just about one specific thing. All of these little factors fit together like a very complex puzzle.

Not a beginner's puzzle either, one of those 10,000 piece monstrosities that takes an army to understand.

You can't just eat good food and call it a day. (I truly wish it was that easy.) Eating well will only account for a portion of your mood. It'll help with the balancing of your neurochemicals and assist you with your toxic-thought management, but these thoughts won't go away unless you actively work on cleansing them from your brain.

And when you're recovering from a traumatic experience such as a toxic childhood home, or a prolonged abusive relationship, intrusive thoughts are a side effect. Almost a form of flashbacks, but more intense because they can feel like your *own* thoughts.

And they aren't even blatantly malicious thoughts either...

Let me explain.

First of all, spending a half decade (or more for some of you reading, and I am so sorry for that) being told that you are fat, lazy, stupid, and ugly FUCKS YOU UP!!! And in ways that you didn't even know existed.

Even when you don't consciously believe what you are being told, it starts to reprogram your subconscious brain.

Remember that really heavy frog analogy from the first chapter?

I'm going to reiterate it anyways:

If you place a frog in a pot of boiling water, they will react to the great by jumping out of the pot to save their own lives.

BUT

**_If you place a frog in a pot of cold water and then turn the
heat up, the gradual introduction of the threat will cause
the frog to stay in the water and die (accidentally killing
itself.)_**

A BIT WORDIER THAN the first time, but I cannot stress enough
that the second frog **_DIES._**

It's the same with an abusive relationship. The abusee is the frog,
and the relationship is the pot of water. The abuser would be the hand
cruel enough to turn on the heat and kill the frog. Your brain starts to
change when you are subtly berated all the time.

NOW, AS YOU KNOW BY now, I am not a medical professional
and only have direct, personal experience from my own journey. **If you
are struggling, please seek professional help. This book is in now
way, shape or form intended to replace the advice or guidance of a
trained and licensed professional.**

But...

Keeping that in mind, this is what I personally experienced.

ON THE SURFACE I KNEW that the main things I was told were
not true. I may have been overweight and unhealthy from eating fast
food every day, but I also actively moved my body. I knew how to call
out that lie. I didn't associate myself with the term "fat." I wasn't lazy,
I went to school, maintained good grades, and worked a laborious job
after school. I knew how to call out that lie.

I struggle with not feeling stupid on and off, because I've always been really smart, like a dead ringer for "Hermione Granger," but after being dinged up over the years, I do have occasional issues with memory recall, impulse control, and all that.

Despite being super smart, I need things repeated for me and get confused easily. But, associating as "stupid" doesn't do me any good, and those feelings would only really creep up in my conscious mind in moments of extreme despair, as an afterthought.

"I wasted the food because I dropped it, broke that dish, … … yeah and you're stupid too."

In the beginning, it can be tricky to break these patterns. And the first step in that is admitting that you have patterns that need to be broken.

I used to journal when I was having an episode. That way I could get the toxic words out of my mind without speaking them into being. Because when we speak, words are given life.

Even while writing this chapter, it is difficult for me to type the toxic words, because they are simply not true, and not anything that anyone ever deserves to be told.

I have a notebook in my burn pile FILLED with my negative thoughts from when I was just starting out my healing journey. As soon as I would obsess over the darkness welling within me like a new spring bubbling up, I would ferociously journal.

The experience was always trance-like. I wouldn't think about the thoughts that I was writing, but would more so channel them; letting them float through the pen rather than bounce around in my mind.

And what I experienced truly surprised me...

... I found that eventually, it did have a stopping point. That eventually, I would "snap to," coming out of my "trance," wondering why I had lost my train of thought before looking back to see how many pages I had filled with hate — detoxing it from my soul.

It was ALARMING at times. Especially to "wake up" so to speak feeling level headed and refreshingly naive. But that's what happened, without fail, every single time I decided to journal my way through the intrusive thoughts.

And eventually, it got to the point where I didn't have anything left to purge (in that way).

Actually, the reason why I've dedicated myself to sharing what I've been through is to let you know that this is only the beginning of your healing journey, and not a cure all. More important than the extent of your wounds is the extent of your dedication to healing.

So, before we move on and talk about how your beliefs will limit your trajectory if you are not careful, I need to know...

Do you ever feel badly about yourself?

Do you ever feel too "this" or too "that"?

Do you ever think that you are undeserving of what you want out of life?

If so, find a notebook, separate from the one you use for the other exercises. A notebook that you promise NEVER to read and will safely burn once it has completed its mission.

And the next time you feel toxic thoughts bubble up, journal them until you can stop — until they stop spilling over. Then take a mental note of how you feel after the fact.

Do you feel relieved?

Do you feel cleansed?

Do you feel grounded, centered, and whole?

That was MY experience...

And I hope that you feel the same.

Now, moving on to the lies we tell ourselves...

I've never been officially diagnosed with PTSD, but I have done enough research to feel confident that it is something I have lived with and overcome, for the most part.

However...

There was a period in my life when I thought that this would mean that I was doomed to live a fucked up eternity. Granted, at that time I had other things going on in my life such as inconsistent eating habits and the fact that I wasn't nurturing my brain yet, BUT...

Looking back. I can see a direct correlation between when I was actively associating myself with PTSD and the number of my episodes as well as the severity of my symptoms.

In simple terms, I was a wreck.

I blamed my life and behaviors on my abuse and held onto that limiting belief for quite some time. To the point of not taking control of my episodes.

"Oh, I have PTSD, I can't help it..."

Needless to say, this caused a lot of undue stress in my relationship with Pumpkin.

And I talk about it now because throughout my life I have had a lot of experience with people who assumed any relationship problems we had were his fault. When in reality, recovery is MESSY and I was feeding myself <u>lies</u>.

What you say to yourself **matters**.

If you spend all of your time associating yourself with being broken or damaged, you WILL live a broken, damaged life. No questions asked.

That's right, no questions asked.

It doesn't matter if you have the nicest house and the best car with the most compatible relationship, if you tell yourself that you are broken and damaged, your brain will look for the evidence to support that.

"You say that your life is destined to be a rollercoaster ride of mood swings?... You got it boss!"

"You say that everyone in your life will only hurt or manipulate you? We should probably go make friends with that toxic troll over there. By the way, did you hear what they said about you??"

We create our own realities.

From the people we surround ourselves with to the jobs we get in life, it's all from the patterns that have been programmed into your brain.

It's not just about what you want to manifest. It's also about what you **don't** want.

When you're constantly thinking about the things you **_don't_** want to experience, you're still putting a heck of a lot of energy into that thing, and that energy brings it to fruition.

And, the worst part is, we have been trained to believe that these things are out of our control. That we have to live with the cards we are dealt and to just deal with it.

But that is simply *not true*.

Once I identified this behavior within myself, I stopped living my life as a tragedy.

And that's not to say that my mindset shifts stopped my flashbacks or healed my triggers, I definitely had to work on those issues separately. But, changing my attitude from one fixed on suffering to one focused on the growth that happens from healing, I was able to be at peace with my flashbacks, accept them for what they were, and work through them.

I am no longer defined by what happened to me.

I no longer allow my past to restrict my potential.

Currently, I am living fully in the moment in order to face my trauma, heal from it, and move forward to become a *superhero*.

A goddess.

And it is because I caught myself in a loop of keeping myself damaged because I benefited from the excuse that I didn't have any more growing to do and was simply the way I was.

But that loop nearly cost me my relationship, several times.

A relationship that gives me a reason to live.

A relationship that gives me a reason to be my best self.

We all go through moments of darkness so that we can see the light shine.

And it is because I went through these moments of darkness that I am so passionate about sharing the light that I found with you — because I don't want you to be forced to go through those moments of darkness alone, or thinking that things will always be this way.

That's not to say that certain situations and people are for you when they are not, because that's not the case at all. If you are considering that a certain person or situation is wrong for you, meditate on it, listen to your intuition, and walk away when necessary.

I only managed to resolve the issues in my relationship because it is a true fit. If we weren't meant for each other, it would have fallen apart at some point.

Relationship status as aide, the important thing is that if you don't create a narrative for yourself in which you are losing, *you'll win*.

You will only ever be as healthy, successful, and abundant as your imagination allows you to be.

I will say that again...

You will only ever be as healthy, successful, and abundant as your imagination allows you to be.

It is all entirely up to you, and always has been.

Today, I want you to identify your limiting beliefs by writing them down.

It's scary, and a little painful, but facing these self proclaimed obstacles will help you to dissolve them.

First, think of an issue.

Are you causing drama in your relationships? Are you dissatisfied with your rate? Are you frustrated with your pay rate at your job?

Do you make excuses for that thing?

What are those excuses?

Are you broke because you come from a poor family?
Do you have someone specific in mind that you can blame for your shortcomings?

Write it down.

Let it aaallll out.

Got it?

Good.

Now, take that list of excuses and create a new list out of it.

Start a line with "I am unhindered by," and then write one of your excuses to finish the sentence.

FOR EXAMPLE, MINE WOULD be:

**I am unhindered by my previous relationships.*
**I am unhindered by my traumatic experiences.*
**I am unhindered by my PTSD.*
(And so forth.)

What are you ***unhindered*** by, Goddess?

The second half of this book is filled with affirmations for your mental stability and overall prosperity, but right now, I want you to say the following phrases out loud:

- ★ *The present is not dictated by my past.*
- ★ *I am fully capable of living a peaceful, stable existence.*
- ★ *I fully deserve everything my heart desires.*
- ★ *I am worth of my heart's desires*
- ★ *Thank you, thank you, thank you, and so it is.*

The human mind is an incredible thing.
How will you use it to create your reality?

Chapter Six - The Power of What We Think (Part Two)

Before we move onto the fun part – the affirmations to help you raise your vibration, I want to take a second to talk about how the power of what we think affects each other.

Everything that we do has a personal impact, as well as a **collective** impact. And it's important to be aware of that aspect of life.

I've had *two* conversations in recent years that led me to write this chapter of the book, because it is *that* important.

When I was a kid, I didn't have many female companions. There was always this bitter sense of rivalry with the other girls when I was younger. It was always a lot less of supporting each other and a lot more tearing each other down and using each other. So, unfortunately, I *understand* where the woman I encountered was coming from... but it's just *so* sad.

I ENCOUNTERED A WOMAN recently who asked what I write, to which I honestly replied, "fiction for women."

To my surprise, she found the specification *disheartening* and said that I shouldn't limit myself to just women.

Regardless of what anyone can tell me, helping women is what my soul wants to do. Goddesses are my soul tribe and no one's opinion will ever change the fact that I write *for* **women**. I love to imagine the different women who will pick up a copy of one of my books and relate with one of my leading ladies in one way or another.

But this woman felt differently.

She told me that as a bartender she had met enough women to "know that women are horrible."

This thought process *hurts* the Goddess collective. Like... really truly injures the collective.

When a woman is of the belief that other women are horrible, she closes herself off subconsciously to the possibility of any kind of sisterly relationship. In fact, she tears down the integrity of the sisterhood. AND, by generalizing all women as "horrible" she is also tearing herself down, inherently stating that there are parts of herself that are horrible because she is a woman.

It is all very problematic.

And sad.

And I hate to admit... I used to be this way.

Truthfully, I never imagined that I would *want* to connect women to help uplift them.

...WHEN I WAS IN THE SIXTH grade, I chose Gone with the Wind for a book report. (*sigh, face-palm*) It was due after Christmas break (and I ended up needing to take a couple of days off from school to finish reading the behemoth book because it is OVER 1,000 pages long.)

I related a lot to Scarlett O'Hara, the book's protagonist, quite a bit because she was beautiful and the other women hated her for it. I now refer to that mindset as "Scarlett O'Hara Syndrome" because it was *so* pertinent to her narrative.

Gone with the Wind was published in 1936 by Margaret Mitchell. (As I mentioned) it was over 1K pages, and has two sequels that I have never read, written by various authors. It really speaks to Margaret Mitchell's work that her story was vivid enough to be carried on by two separate authors on two separate occasions; and that it held my attention at the age of 11 despite being written decades earlier.

It is set in the civil war, but it is riveting.

Gone with the Wind was made into a film three years after publication, in 1939. Admittedly, I wanted to read the book because I had QUITE the crush on Rhett Butler from the movie who was a suave man who treated women like (*ahem*) equals, acted on his passions, and stood up for what he believed in... even if it made him a bit of a misogynist.

Rhett Butler was NOT the healthiest image of how a man should treat the woman in his life, especially at an early age. Sure, he was *suave,* but looking back, he is definitely not a character that anyone should be crushing on.

And that is exactly the point that I want to make before we move on.

Since at *LEAST* the 1930's women have had such terrible experiences with other women that they would rather be mistreated by men, AND it became the theme for a THOUSAND PAGE book!!

So, let's take a moment to talk about generational trauma.

Margaret Mitchell wrote about this experience in a setting **60-75** years before her time, because it is set in the Civil War through the Reconstruction Era. **60-75 years previous... as if it was a story told by her grandmother.**

And *I* read this book approximately **70 years later**.

Let that sink in for a moment, because it is fucking nuts.

For over 140 YEARS, we've been carrying around this narrative that other women are bitches, in a mainstream way.

140 YEARS!!!

And because it is historical fiction it is easy to blur the lines and believe it to be true.

140 YEARS!!!!!!!

takes a deep breath

This is a toxin that our grandmother's *grandmother's* **GRANDMOTHER'S** were poisoned with.

And it ate away at ALL of us so that NONE of us could trust each other.

I have known **COUNTLESS** women who have told me that they have lots of guy friends because they don't get along with women.

WHY????

Because for over _**140 YEARS**_ we have been told to hate each other. That self isolation is far better than trusting other women.

THAT'S 1.4 <u>CENTURIES</u>!!!

Goddess...

We have to stop this epidemic.

We are abusing ourselves by isolating ourselves so much. By destroying the idea of a sisterhood, we only destroy ourselves.

It is a plight to our society. And when we overcome this disgusting "every woman for herself" mentality, we will change the world.

Together, we WILL change the world!

AND OF _course_ that's not to say that you will always vibe with every other female on the face of the planet. Of course not.

But you can't generalize and say that ALL women are horrible. It hurts your self-image. Yes, there are people on different frequencies, but what good does it do for you to talk shit on others?

...

...

...

And it all goes back to "ego mindset."

"Scarlett O'Hara Syndrome" _is_ "ego mindset." You can be beautiful without being enemies with all the women around you.

We cannot sit around and peck away at each other like vultures anymore.

AND IF YOU ARE HOLDING this in your hands reading this and thinking down on yourself because you feel guilty about doing this recently — GOOD!

I am glad that this is getting through to you.

But **STOP** feeling down on yourself because I used to be there too.

IT WASN'T UNTIL THE universe sent me an angel who cherishes female relationships in her own life that I saw the need for it in my own life. And our paths have since diverged once more, but she reminded me of the importance for women to connect, and that is why I am here.

I said I'd had *two* conversations recently that prompted this chapter.

The second conversation is actually a recurring one, whenever anyone asks why I am just focused on writing for and working with women.

The answer is pretty simple.

We have been isolated for centuries, and it is finally time to come together and heal from that.

It is time to come together and heal from this generational toxin.

So, today's exercise is also "pretty simple."

Have a heartfelt conversation with at least *two* important women in your life today. (Yes two.)

Go forth after putting this book down and strengthen the relationships that you have with the women in your life, because it is time to come together and heal.

If you are looking to connect with other Goddesses worldwide, head to the link at the back of this book to join my forum, a private space specifically for us to come together and heal.

And, if you haven't already, head over to my bookshop and pick up a copy of <u>Note to Self</u>, which is FULL of affirmations and exercises to help you stay grounded in your Goddess energy.

Part Two – Becoming a Goddess

What is the "Goddess Frame of Mind?"

The Goddess Frame of Mind is the mentality that you are in control of your own reality. Simply put, it is connecting your earthbound consciousness with your cosmic higher self so that you can create the reality that you want.

Being a Goddess is a state of mind.

To achieve this mindset, you must be aware of the "bigger picture" because you cannot connect to your higher self with a closed mind. The Goddess Frame of Mind is the divine state of knowing and believing that you can accomplish anything you put your mind to.

Being a Goddess means taking the time to incorporate these seven foundational practices into your day to day life:

- ★ Self care routines
- ★ Meditation
- ★ Cooking with whole foods
- ★ Spending time in nature
- ★ Taking action steps towards goals
- ★ Being your best authentic self
- ★ Believing in your dreams

Ego v. Goddess Mentality

I wasn't able to fully transcend out of ego-driven mindset and into the Goddess Frame of Mind until I was 25, going on 26 years old. That was only a couple of years ago.

I was uncomfortable in my own skin. I felt like I was running in place. And overall, I felt downright defeated.

I didn't even realize that I was *addressing* my ego-driven mentality when I was able to shift out of it. I switched out of ego mindset when I shifted from "scarcity" to "abundance" mindset.

See, the scarcity mindset is an extension of the ego. The ego is driven by **greed** and **competition**, and is also **self-isolating**. Meanwhile, an abundance mindset is an extension of the higher self, or your inner Goddess.

Having an abundance mindset means that you believe that there is enough room at the table for everyone and there is enough food to go around and then some. It is the belief that everyone deserves to succeed, and is most certainly welcome to do so.

You cannot switch out of the scarcity mindset without also shedding the ego mentality and stepping into your cosmic light.

Surprisingly, I never realized that all my fear and anxiety over not being able to succeed because other people around me *were* succeeding was ego driven. Modern society would like to program you to *believe* that there is not enough room at the table. And that is something that will always inhibit your self-worth from fully manifesting.

I was focused on healing my self-worth and stepping out of the thoughts that there is not enough metaphorical food to go around when I also stepped out of my ego and into my higher self as a result.

The two go hand in hand.

It is not easy to let go of your ego. She has tricked you into thinking she knows what feels good for a lonnnnngg time. But, when you stop focusing on her and find ways to better the other aspects of yourself, soon you'll forget why you needed Ego in the first place.

What Are Affirmations?

We talked about it here and there in the first half of the book, but you deserve to fully understand what affirmations are, how to use them, and how to create them for yourself.

Affirmations are believable statements to be said out loud repetitiously in order to rewire the way your brain thinks.

It sounds so silly at first, but there is legitimate science behind it. You know why? It's the same tactic that your abuser used to get you to the point you're at now, only in reverse.

The monster of your past repeated statements that you believed were untrue until they became fact in your reality, affecting how you function in your day to day life.

Affirmations allow you to take that power back by repeating positive things to yourself until they become fact in your reality, ultimately affecting how you function in your day to day life, but for your highest and greatest good and harming none.

How To Use Affirmations?

Affirmations are a very simple, powerful tool that you can access for free. At first, you may have some hesitation towards the process, but push through the negative thoughts and build a routine around repeating your affirmations daily.

Affirmations are best used in repetition. You should repeat each phrase 3-5 times in a row. And you should make time for affirmations 3-5 times a week, preferably 3-5 times a *day* as well.

The amount of time you spend with your affirmations will vary on what you are doing with them. But just know that, the more dedicated you are to them, the more powerful they become.

HOW DO I WRITE MY OWN Affirmations?

Very good and important question.

Before you dive into the affirmations that *I* have created for you, you should know how to write your own affirmations.

Writing your own affirmations is very simple.

You simply write an "I" statement that is in-tune with your goals.

Affirmations can be as simple as, "I am beautiful," and, "I am loved." They can also be as complex as, "I am worthy of being a bestselling author."

The beauty of creating your own affirmations is that you can cater them entirely to your personality, your circumstances, and the things that you wish to manifest in your life.

Incantations

Believe it or not, incantations are a very real and incredibly powerful way to boost your healing journey.

When you hear the word "incantation," images of pointy hats and bubbling cauldrons likely pop up in your head. I was surprised when I was first introduced to the more relatable concept of incantations in my mindset coaching courses.

Incantations are when you add powerful gestures and movements to your affirmations.

Simple as that.

If you start *dancing* while you chant your affirmations, the impact of what you're saying increases, making it easier for you to believe it as fact and begin putting your goals into action to make your dreams a reality.

The easiest way to begin doing this is to start choosing powerful songs with "I am" statements in the lyrics so that you can sing and dance along and embody the power of those lyrics.

Once you get comfortable with the concept you will find yourself stomping out a beat and fist pumping to your own affirmations, creating powerful incantations that will help to cement your words in this reality.

<u>Goddess Affirmations</u>

I have compiled a handful of affirmations for you in order to help you raise your vibration and help you achieve the things that you want in life.

Each affirmation should take approximately 10-15 minutes to complete, and the approximate times are listed at the beginning of each chapter.

Create a sacred space where you will be able to complete the exercise undisturbed.

Take a few deep breaths, and then, slowly repeat each phrase out loud.

Take your time. This is about connecting with your higher self and enjoying the process.

You may find that you end the session in a dreamy state of being. Allow yourself to come out of the afterglow gradually so that you can fully enjoy the progress of your cosmic journey.

IF YOU WOULD PREFER a guided meditation experience, go to the link at the back of the book and check out the Goddess Frame of Mind podcast, where you can find recorded versions of each of these affirmations.

Affirmations for Renewal (approx. 15 minutes)

I shed the layers of my past so that I may fly into my highest vibration of being.
I shed the layers of my past so that I may fly into my highest vibration of being.
I shed the layers of my past so that I may fly into my highest vibration of being.

I am ready to step into a better reality.
I am ready to step into a better reality.
I am ready to step into a better reality.

I deserve to create the reality I desire.
I deserve to create the reality I desire.
I deserve to create the reality I desire.

May this year fulfill my every goal.
May this year fulfill my every goal.
May this year fulfill my every goal.

I am capable of anything I put my mind to.
I am capable of anything I put my mind to.
I am capable of anything I put my mind to.

I am worthy of receiving all I desire, and more.
I am worthy of receiving all I desire, and more.
I am worthy of receiving all I desire, and more.

I thank the universe for my past challenges which have made me
stronger, and am ready for the path ahead.
I thank the universe for my past challenges which have made me
stronger, and am ready for the path ahead.
I thank the universe for my past challenges which have made me
stronger, and am ready for the path ahead.

I welcome the constant cycle of renewal in life.
I welcome the constant cycle of renewal in life.
I welcome the constant cycle of renewal in life.

I am a phoenix. I shall always rise again.
I am a phoenix. I shall always rise again.
I am a phoenix. I shall always rise again.

I am a pure being of love and light.
I am a pure being of love and light.
I am a pure being of love and light.

I am worthy of achieving my goals.

I am worthy of achieving my goals.

I am worthy of achieving my goals.

I am capable of manifesting my dreams.
I am capable of manifesting my dreams.
I am capable of manifesting my dreams.

I am renewed.
I am renewed.
I am renewed.

Thank you
Thank you
Thank you
And so it is.

AFFIRMATIONS TO PROMOTE *Unconditional Self-Love*
(approx. 10 minutes)

I am whole and complete as I am.
I am whole and complete as I am.
I am whole and complete as I am.

Everything I need lives within me.
Everything I need lives within me.
Everything I need lives within me.

I am beautiful.
I am beautiful.
I am beautiful.

I love every inch of my being, inside and out.
I love every inch of my being, inside and out.
I love every inch of my being, inside and out.

I accept my flaws as part of my perfection.
I accept my flaws as part of my perfection.
I accept my flaws as part of my perfection.

The lessons I've learned from my mistakes add to my beauty.
The lessons I've learned from my mistakes add to my beauty.
The lessons I've learned from my mistakes add to my beauty.

Beautiful is not an aesthetic, it is a frame of mind.
Beautiful is not an aesthetic, it is a frame of mind.
Beautiful is not an aesthetic, it is a frame of mind.

I am a radiant being of love and light.
I am a radiant being of love and light.
I am a radiant being of love and light.

I love myself fully and unconditionally.
I love myself fully and unconditionally.
I love myself fully and unconditionally.

I grow more beautiful each and every day.

I grow more beautiful each and every day.
I grow more beautiful each and every day.

I love myself, and acknowledge the growth I have made along my
journey.
I love myself, and acknowledge the growth I have made along my
journey.
I love myself and acknowledge the growth I have made along my
journey.

When I love myself, the thoughts of others become meaningless.
When I love myself, the thoughts of others become meaningless.
When I love myself, the thoughts of others become meaningless.

I am here to fulfill my dreams.
I am here to fulfill my dreams.
I am here to fulfill my dreams.

Thank you
Thank you
Thank you
And so it is.

AFFIRMATIONS FOR ABUNDANCE (approx. 10 minutes)

I am a cosmic daughter, made of stars, and capable of anything.
I am a cosmic daughter, made of stars, and capable of anything.
I am a cosmic daughter, made of stars, and capable of anything.

I am worthy of all I desire.
I am worthy of all I desire.
I am worthy of all I desire.

I am all that I desire.
I am all that I desire.
I am all that I desire.

I am platinum, silver, and gold.
I am platinum, silver, and gold.
I am platinum, silver, and gold.

I am all that I desire.
I am all that I desire.
I am all that I desire.

I am worthy of health, wealth, and well being.
I am worthy of health, wealth, and well being.
I am worthy of health, wealth, and well being.

I am worthy of all I desire.
I am worthy of all I desire.
I am worthy of all I desire.

I am the chosen one, good things happen for me.
I am the chosen one, good things happen for me.
I am the chosen one, good things happen for me.

I am worthy of living my dreams.
I am worthy of living my dreams.
I am worthy of living my dreams.

I am everything I need and more.
I am everything I need and more.
I am everything I need and more.

I am worthy of love, I am worthy of peace, I am worthy of happiness.
I am worthy of love, I am worthy of peace, I am worthy of happiness.
I am worthy of love, I am worthy of peace, I am worthy of happiness.

I am worthy of all that I desire.
I am worthy of all that I desire.
I am worthy of all that I desire.

I am a Queen, I embody divine riches.
I am a Queen, I embody divine riches.
I am a Queen, I embody divine riches.

I ask the universe for what I want and am open to receiving what is for
my greatest and highest good and harming none.
I ask the universe for what I want and am open to receiving what is for
my greatest and highest good and harming none.
I ask the universe for what I want and am open to receiving what is for
my greatest and highest good and harming none.

I am the chosen one, good things happen for me.
I am the chosen one, good things happen for me.
I am the chosen one, good things happen for me.

I am worthy of fulfilling my destiny.
I am worthy of fulfilling my destiny.
I am worthy of fulfilling my destiny.

I am worthy of achieving my goals.
I am worthy of achieving my goals.
I am worthy of achieving my goals.

I am worthy of all I desire and more.
I am worthy of all I desire and more.
I am worthy of all I desire and more.

I am worthy of love, life, and longevity.
I am worthy of love, life, and longevity.
I am worthy of love, life, and longevity.

I evoke my innate Goddess energy to magnify my worth.
I evoke my innate Goddess energy to magnify my worth.
I evoke my innate Goddess energy to magnify my worth.

I am all I desire.
I am all I desire.
I am all I desire.

I am everything I need and more.
I am everything I need and more.
I am everything I need and more.

I am a Queen, I embody divine riches.
I am a Queen, I embody divine riches.
I am a Queen, I embody divine riches.

I am platinum, I am silver, I am gold.
I am platinum, I am silver, I am gold.
I am platinum, I am silver, I am gold.

I am rubies, I am sapphires, I am emeralds, I am gold.
I am rubies, I am sapphires, I am emeralds, I am gold.
I am rubies, I am sapphires, I am emeralds, I am gold.

I am precious.
I am precious.
I am precious.

I am worthy.
I am worthy.
I am worthy.

I am a cosmic daughter, made of stars, and capable of anything.
I am a cosmic daughter, made of stars, and capable of anything.
I am a cosmic daughter, made of stars, and capable of anything.

Thank you
Thank you
Thank you
And so it is.

AFFIRMATIONS TO MANIFEST Money (approx. 11 minutes)

I am a cosmic treasure.
I am a cosmic treasure.
I am a cosmic treasure.

I am the divine embodiment of abundance.
I am the divine embodiment of abundance.
I am the divine embodiment of abundance.

What is for me shall find its way to me.
What is for me shall find its way to me.
What is for me shall find its way to me.

I am a cosmic treasure.
I am a cosmic treasure.
I am a cosmic treasure.

I am worthy of fulfilling my destiny.
I am worthy of fulfilling my destiny.
I am worthy of fulfilling my destiny.

I am worthy of all that my heart desires.

I am worthy of all that my heart desires.
I am worthy of all that my heart desires.

I am the chosen one, good things happen for me.
I am the chosen one, good things happen for me.
I am the chosen one, good things happen for me.

I am capable of manifesting my dreams.
I am capable of manifesting my dreams.
I am capable of manifesting my dreams.

I am **worthy** of manifesting my dreams.
I am **worthy** of manifesting my dreams.
I am **worthy** of manifesting my dreams.

I am a cosmic treasure.
I am a cosmic treasure.
I am a cosmic treasure.

I am the divine embodiment of abundance.
I am the divine embodiment of abundance.
I am the divine embodiment of abundance.

I live a life of luxury and comfort.
I live a life of luxury and comfort.

I live a life of luxury and comfort.

I live a life of luxury and comfort.
I live a life of luxury and comfort.
I live a life of luxury and comfort.

I live a life of luxury and comfort.
I live a life of luxury and comfort.
I live a life of luxury and comfort.

I am the chosen one, good things happen for me.
I am the chosen one, good things happen for me.
I am the chosen one, good things happen for me.

I am the chosen one, good things happen for me.
I am the chosen one, good things happen for me.
I am the chosen one, good things happen for me.

All of my needs are met, easily without question.
All of my needs are met, easily without question.
All of my needs are met, easily without question.

The universe protects my cosmic treasures.
The universe protects my cosmic treasures.
The universe protects my cosmic treasures.

The universe protects my cosmic treasures.
The universe protects my cosmic treasures.
The universe protects my cosmic treasures.

I am a cosmic treasure.
I am a cosmic treasure.
I am a cosmic treasure.

I am precious metals and rare gems.
I am precious metals and rare gems.
I am precious metals and rare gems.

My soul is platinum, silver, and gold.
My soul is platinum, silver, and gold.
My soul is platinum, silver, and gold.

My aura radiates and magnetizes diamonds, rubies, emeralds, and sapphires.
My aura radiates and magnetizes diamonds, rubies, emeralds, and sapphires.
My aura radiates and magnetizes diamonds, rubies, emeralds, and sapphires.

I am the divine embodiment of abundance.

I am the divine embodiment of abundance.
I am the divine embodiment of abundance.

I am the divine embodiment of abundance.
I am the divine embodiment of abundance.
I am the divine embodiment of abundance.

I am the divine embodiment of abundance.
I am the divine embodiment of abundance.
I am the divine embodiment of abundance.

I am worthy of manifesting my dreams.
I am worthy of manifesting my dreams.
I am worthy of manifesting my dreams.

I am worthy of manifesting my dreams.
I am worthy of manifesting my dreams.
I am worthy of manifesting my dreams.

I am worthy of fulfilling my destiny.
I am worthy of fulfilling my destiny.
I am worthy of fulfilling my destiny.

I am the chosen one, good things happen for me.
I am the chosen one, good things happen for me.

I am the chosen one, good things happen for me.

I am the divine embodiment of abundance.
I am the divine embodiment of abundance.
I am the divine embodiment of abundance.

I am a cosmic treasure.
I am a cosmic treasure.
I am a cosmic treasure.

I am worthy of all I desire.
I am worthy of all I desire.
I am worthy of all I desire.
I am worthy of all I desire.
I am worthy of all I desire.
I am worthy of all I desire.

Thank you
Thank you
Thank you
And so it is.

<u>GODDESS ACTIVATION</u> Affirmation

Alright, Goddess, this is where our time together comes to a close, even though it is just the beginning of your journey.

I would like to leave you with this extra affirmation to help you activate your Goddess energy, any time you are feeling a little zapped, shaky, or unsure of yourself.

There is no audio to go along with this one, so I highly recommend you give yourself 20 minutes to do this affirmation.

OR, you can pick a section of these Goddess Activation Affirmations and say 3 of them, three times over, if you need a quick boost in the middle of a busy day.

Thank you so much for being here Goddess. I love you so much, and I appreciate your willingness to put the work in to achieve your Goddess status.

Until next time, may peace, love, light, and happiness, always be with you.

I am a divine Goddess.
I am a divine Goddess.
I am a divine Goddess.

I am a radiant sunray.
I am a radiant sunray.
I am a radiant sunray.

I am an enchanting moonbeam.
I am an enchanting moonbeam.
I am an enchanting moonbeam.

I pull the tides.
I pull the tides.
I pull the tides.

I am worthy!
I am worthy!
I am worthy!

I am a Goddess and the world is my oyster.
I am a Goddess and the world is my oyster.
I am a Goddess and the world is my oyster.

I am the chosen one, good things happen for me.
I am the chosen one, good things happen for me.
I am the chosen one, good things happen for me.

Whatever is coming next is better than what has left me.
Whatever is coming next is better than what has left me.
Whatever is coming next is better than what has left me.

Abundant opportunities come my way, often.
Abundant opportunities come my way, often.
Abundant opportunities come my way, often.

I am protected by, provided for, and supported by the strength and love of the universe.
I am protected by, provided for, and supported by the strength and love of the universe.
I am protected by, provided for, and supported by the strength and love of the universe.

Thank you
Thank you
Thank you
And so it is.

Don't miss out!

Visit the website below and you can sign up to receive emails whenever Eirian Naomi Omid publishes a new book. There's no charge and no obligation.

https://books2read.com/r/B-A-JLOJ-QXPIC

BOOKS2READ

Connecting independent readers to independent writers.

Did you love *The Goddess Frame of Mind*? Then you should read *Note to Self*[1] by Eirian Naomi Omid et al.!

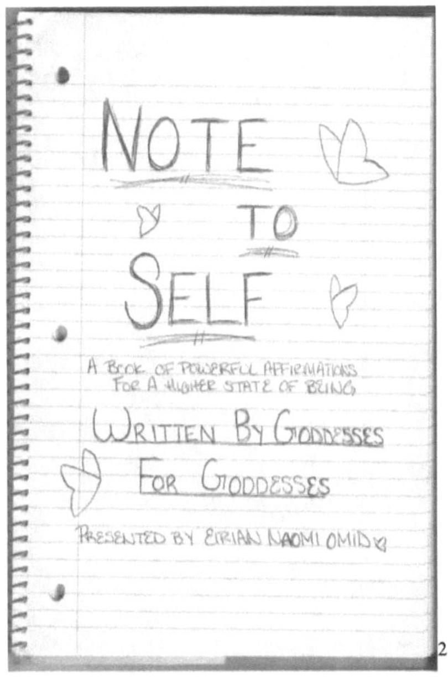

Welcome, Goddess,

We're glad this book found you.

Inside this book, you'll find prayers, meditations, spells, and exercises to help you achieve a higher, more balanced state of being.

Some of the affirmations, prayers, and quotes within have been collected from the Goddess Crowd, Eirian's tribe. It is an honor to present this book to you, Goddess. Your life changes today.

And it starts, with you.

---

1. https://books2read.com/u/3JXNEX

2. https://books2read.com/u/3JXNEX

Also by Eirian Naomi Omid

Faerie Lit
Did You Hear About the Prinz Party?: A Collection of Grimm
Themed Shorts
Asleep For Days
Flashbacks and Afterglow

Finding New Haven
Finding New Haven

Keoni Magnolia
#SelfishSunday

PNK KanD Project
Breakout

Standalone
Note to Self

The Goddess Frame of Mind

Watch for more at https://www.eirianwrites.com/.

About the Author

Eirian Naomi Omid was born and raised in the Gallatin Valley and is the survivor of teenage relationship abuse. As a result, this cosmic faerie is on a mission to help spread love and light to all who need it.

Eirian Naomi has innumerable titles across several book series, all within the speculative literature genre. She is also known to publish inspirational self-help books focused on affirmations on the side; and is currently most proud of her PNK KanD Project - an extensive book series with original music to go with each book that is written and performed by the author herself.

This cosmic faerie is a certified life and mindset coach who delights in helping all of the Sugar Plums on the planet discover, heal, and step into their highest state of being, for a better self, and a better world.

Discover all of the things Eirian Naomi has for what ails you at her homebase: www.eirianwrites.com

Read more at https://www.eirianwrites.com/.

About the Publisher

EirianWrites Studios is a multi-media company specializing in written word as well as audio and visual content.

Founded in 2021, EirianWrites Studio prides itself on innovating the ever changing entertainment industry by providing you with new and exciting experiences, and new ways to fully immerse yourself into what you are reading.

Rep your favorite fictional brands. Head over to the EirianWrites Boutique today!